Korean MP3 Audio Files for This Book Available at

newampersand.com/beautifulstory

Beautiful Short Stories in English and Korean - Bilingual / Dual Language Picture Book for Beginners

Story by Hye-min Choi

ISBN 9791188195473

For permission requests, write us at marketing@newampersand.com

Ordering Information:

Special discounts are available on quantity purchases
by corporations, associations, and others.

For details, contact the publisher at the email address above.

Printed in the United States of America

www.newampersand.com

내가 어렸을때
When I Was Little

내가 어렸을때,
When I was little,

모든 것이 신기해 보였어요.
Everything looked amazing.

아빠는 힘이 세고, 엄마는 요리를 잘했어요.
My daddy was strong, and my mom could cook well.

나도 어른이 되고싶다!
I want to become a grown-up, too!

어른이 되면 어떤 멋진 일들이 생길까?
If I become a grown-up, what kind of cool things would happen?

나는 이제 어른이 되었어요.
I became a grown-up now.

어른으로 사는 것은 정말 피곤해!
Living as a grown-up is really tiring!

아침 일찍 회사에 가고, 저녁 늦게 집에오지.
I go to work early in the morning and come back home late at night.

아! 다시 어린이가 되고싶다!
Oh! I wish to become a child again!

꿈속에서
In The Dream

어제 밤에 꿈을 꾸었어요.
I had a dream last night.

나의 몸에 날개가 달려있었어요.
I had wings attached to my body.

하늘 높이 올라가서, 아래를 보았어요.
I went up in the sky and looked down.

모든 것들이 작게 보였어요.
Everything looked small.

장난감 같이 작은 사람들.
People, that are small like toys.

솜사탕 같은 구름!
The cloud, which is like cotton candy!

구름에 앉아보려고 했어요.
I tried to sit on the cloud.

하지만, 가까이 다가가니 사라져 버렸어요.
But, they disappeared as I approached nearby.

너무 오래 날아다녀서 피곤해졌어요.
I became tired because I had been flying for too long.

힘이 빠져서 땅으로 떨어진다!
I am losing strength and I'm falling to the ground!

쾅! 아이고 아프다!
Thump! Ouch, it hurts!

침대에서 떨어졌네.
I fell from the bed.

친구가 생겼어요
I Made a Friend

오늘은 정말 기분이 좋아요.
I'm feeling really good today.

학교에서 새로운 친구를 만들었기 때문이에요.
It's because I made a new friend at school.

그 친구의 이름은 선미.
That friend's name is Seon-mi.

나이는 나와 똑같아요.
Her age is exactly the same as mine.

나와 선미는 학교에 같이 다녀요.
I and Seon-mi go to school together.

매일 공부를 같이 할 거예요.
We will study together every day.

선미는 지금 무엇을 하고 있을까?
What might Seon-mi be doing now?

내일은 점심도 같이 먹어야지.
Tomorrow we will have lunch together as well.

나의 가장 친한 친구 선미.
My best friend Seon-mi.

선미와 사이좋게 지낼거예요
I will get along with her.

싸우지 않고.
Without fighting.

우리는 좋은 친구!
We are good friends!

강아지와 고양이
A Puppy and A Cat

멍멍! 이게 무슨 소리야?
Bow-wow! What is this sound?

강아지 소리 같아!
It sounds like a puppy!

어서 소리가 나는 곳으로 가보자.
Let's go to where the sound is coming from.

어머나 세상에!
Oh my goodness!

강아지 두 마리가 있어요.
There are two puppies.

여기에서 무엇을 하고 있지?
What are they doing here?

엄마를 잃어버렸나?
Did they lose their mom?

야옹! 이건 무슨 소리야?
Meow! What is THIS sound?

고양이 소리 아닐까?
Isn't it the sound of a cat?

고양이가 틀림없어!
There's no doubt it's a cat!

우와! 고양이가 강아지들의 엄마인가봐.
Wow! It seems like the cat is the puppies' mom.

고양이가 강아지들을 사랑해!
The cat loves the puppies!

학교에 가자
Let's Go To School

늦었다! 어서 일어나야해.
I'm late! I've got to get up.

오늘은 학교 첫날이예요.
Today is the first day of school.

어떤 친구들을 만날까? 정말 궁금해요.
What kind of friends will I meet? I'm really curious.

키가 큰 친구, 재미있는 친구, 조용한 친구.
A tall friend, a funny friend, a quiet friend.

모두 만나보고 싶어요.
I want to meet them all.

선생님은 어떨까?
What would the teacher be like?

무서운 선생님일까? 자상한 선생님일까?
Would he/she be a scary teacher? A considerate teacher?

학교에 가는 길이 멀지 않게 느껴져요.
The way to school doesn't feel far away.

너무나 즐거운 마음이기 때문이에요.
It's because I'm feeling really joyful.

친구들아! 학교에 가자!
Friends, let's go to school!

공부 하고, 운동도 하고,
Let's study, exercise,

많이 배우자!
and learn a lot!

없어진 지갑
The Missing Wallet

흠, 이상하다. 어디로 갔지?
Hm, this is strange. Where did it go?

무엇을 찾으시나요? 기차 역무원이 물었다.
What are you looking for? The train station staff asked.

분명히 여기에 있던 지갑이 없어졌습니다.
The wallet, which was surely here, has gone missing.

마지막으로 본 것이 언제인가요?
When was the last time you saw it?

약 10분 전, 제가 깜빡 졸기 전에요.
About 10 minutes ago, before I dozed off.

주위에는 누가 있었나요? 생각 해보세요.
Who was there around you? Try to think.

제가 맞게 기억한다면, 저 사람 한명밖에 없었어요.
If I remember correctly, there was only that one person.

지저분한 머리, 냄새나는 옷... 범인이 분명합니다.
Unkempt hair, smelly clothes... He must be the criminal.

실례합니다. 잠깐 가방을 열어주시겠습니까?
Excuse me. Would you please open your bag?

왜 그러시죠? 제가 뭘 잘못했나요?
What's going on? Did I do something wrong?

잠시만 협조를 부탁드립니다.
I ask for your brief cooperation.

여기 있습니다. 잘 보세요. 아무것도 없죠?
Here you are. Look closely. There is nothing, right?

네, 그렇군요. 협조해 주셔서 감사합니다.
Yes, you are right. Thanks for cooperating.

애석하군요! 지갑은 사라진 것 같습니다.
Bummer! Your wallet seems to have disappeared.

정말 세상에는 믿을 사람이 없군요!
There is really no one I can trust in this world!

화가 많이 난 그는 자리에서 일어났다.
He, who was very upset, stood up from the seat.

그리고 그가 앉아있던 자리에, 그의 지갑이 있었다.
And on the seat where he was sitting, was his wallet.

동물원 이야기
The Zoo Story

세상에서 가장 신비로운 곳을 찾는다면, 동물원을 추천한다.
If you are looking for the most magical place in the world,
I'd recommend the zoo.

빠르게 달리는 치타, 아름다운 옷을 입고 있는 공작새,
거대한 코끼리.
A fast-running cheetah, a peacock that's wearing beautiful clothes,
and a gigantic elephant.

상상이 현실이 되는 이 공간. 어린이들의 웃음이 멈추지 않는다.
The place where imagination becomes reality. Kids' laughters don't stop.

동물들은 우리를 바라보며 어떤 생각을 할까?
What would the animals think looking at us?

우리의 대화를 이해 할 수 있을까?
Can they understand our conversations?

동물들에게 먹이를 주지 마세요! 경고문이 보인다.
Do not give food to the animals! I see the warning sign.

몰래 주면 안될까? 배 고파 보이는데.
Can't I give it to them secretly? They look hungry.

우리 집에 같이 갈까? 맛있는 음식이 많은데.
Shall we go to my home together? There are lots of delicious food.

우리는 좋은 친구가 될 것 같아.
I think we will be good friends.

엄마 아빠도 너를 좋아하실거야.
Mom and dad will like you too.

같이 게임을 하고, 산책도 가고.
We will play games together, and take a walk, too.

생각만 해도 정말 즐겁다!
I'm really excited just by thinking!

이제 동물원이 닫을 시간입니다. 안내방송이 들린다.
It's time to close the zoo. I hear an announcement.

오늘은 안되겠다. 다음에 또 올게!
Today won't work. I will be back again next time!

다시 만날때까지 잘 지내!
Take care until we meet again!

-동물들의 대화-
-Conversation between animals-

저 아이가 정말 다시 올까?
Will that kid really come back again?

아니, 집에 가자마자 비디오 게임을 하면서 우리를 잊어버릴거야.
No, he will forget about us as soon as he gets home, playing video games.

그래, 우리도 이제는 익숙해졌어.
Right, we are now used to it.

고양이의 복수
A Cat's Revenge

나는 페르시안 고양이다. 나이는 다섯 살.
I'm a Persian cat. I'm five years old.

나는 인간이라는 생명체와 같이 산다.
I live with a living creature named human.

그는 알아듣지 못할 말을 하고, 이해하기 힘든 행동을 한다.
He says stuff that I can't comprehend and does things that I can't understand.

그의 목적은 무엇일까? 왜 나를 이곳에 데려온 것일까?
What might be his goal? Why did he bring me here?

생각을 계속 하면 의심이 가득해진다.
If I keep thinking, I become full of doubts.

결국에는 나를 해치려고 하겠지?
He will try to hurt me in the end, right?

기다리면 안되겠다. 내가 먼저 행동해야겠어.
I shouldn't wait. I must act first.

저 녀석의 약점을 파악하자. 무엇을 좋아하는지,
무엇을 싫어하는지. 자세히 관찰하자.
Let's analyze what that dude's weaknesses are. What he likes,
and what he hates. Let's observe closely.

저 녀석을 없애버릴 방법을 찾으면, 바로 실행에 옮기자.
If I find a way to get rid of him, I should put it into action immediately.

어서 와서 간식 먹어라! 인간이 나를 부른다.
Come quick and have your snack! The human is calling me.

이럴수가! 내가 가장 좋아하는 생선이잖아!
My god! It's my favorite fish!

그래, 너를 없애려던 나의 계획은 잠시 미뤄두지.
Okay, I will temporarily put off my plan of getting rid of you.

나는 자비로운 고양이니까.
Because I'm a generous cat.

저는 누구일까요?
Who Might I Be?

재미난 놀이를 해 봅시다. 저는 누구일까요?
Let's play a fun game. Who might I be?

힌트를 드릴게요. 잘 생각 해보세요.
I will give you a hint. Think carefully.

나는 다리가 네개 입니다. 옷을 입지 않아요.
I have four legs. I don't wear clothes.

고기는 먹지 않아요. 풀을 먹고 살아요.
I don't eat meat. I eat grass.

머리에 뿔이 나는 친구들도 있어요.
I have some friends who have horns grow on their heads.

걸음은 느립니다. 성격도 느긋하죠.
I am slow-footed. I have an easy-going personality, too.

눈이 크고, 덩치도 큽니다.
My eyes are big, and I have a big body, too.

초원에서 살지만, 인간 가까이에서도 살아요.
I live on the grassland, but I also live near humans.

저의 젖은 인간들의 중요한 음식입니다.
My milk is an important food for humans.

또 한가지 특별한 것이 있어요.
I have another special thing.

저는 위장을 네개 갖고 있어요. 소화를 아주 꼼꼼히 하죠.
I have four stomachs. I digest very thoroughly.

자, 이제 제가 누구인지 알겠죠?
Well, you know who I am by now, right?

보물찾기
Treasure Hunt

그거 알아? 우리 마을의 호수 바닥에, 엄청난 보물이 숨겨져있데.
Did you know that? At the bottom of the lake in our village, there is said to be an enormous treasure hidden.

누가 그래? 그런 것들은 전부 헛소문이야.
Says who? Such things are all false rumors.

아니야! 우리 삼촌이 나에게 얘기해줬어.
Wrong! My uncle told me.

삼촌이 어렸을때, 어떤 사람들이 어두운 밤에 호수에 커다란 상자를 던지던 것을 보았데.
When my uncle was little, he saw some people throwing big boxes into the lake at dark night.

그런데 상자가 열렸고, 안에는 반짝이는 것들이 가득 들어있었데.
And the box opened, and there was a box full of shiny things inside.

그게 무엇일까? 보석? 금화? 왜 호수에 숨겨놨을까?
What would it be? Gemstones? Gold coins?
Why did they hide them in the lake?

정말 궁금하다. 우리가 찾으러 가볼까?
I'm really curious. Shall we go find them?

안돼! 분명히 무시무시한 괴물이 있을거야!
No way! There must be a scary monster!

에이, 너는 정말 겁쟁이구나. 용기가 없어!
Come on, you are a real coward. You have no courage!

그럼 나 혼자 가볼거야. 비밀로 해줘!
Then I will go by myself. Keep it a secret!

알겠어. 하지만 보물을 찾으면 나에게도 조금 줘야해!
Got it. But if you find the treasure, you have to give it to me a little!

당연하지, 내 가장 친한 친구니까.
Of course, because you are my best friend.
보물을 찾으면 무엇을 할까?
What should I do if I find the treasure?

그 돈으로 세계일주를 해야겠다!
I should take a round-the-world trip with the money!

새로운 친구들을 만들고, 멋진 문화를 경험하고.
Make new friends, and experience amazing cultures.

돌아와서 모두에게 이야기 해 줘야지.
I will share it with everyone when I get back.

– 다음날 아침 –
- Next Morning -

엄마! 친구들과 소풍 갈게요.
Mom! I'm going on a picnic with my friends.

그래, 조심히 다녀오거라. 너무 늦지 않게 돌아오고!
Okay, have a safe trip. Come back before it's too late!

한 걸음, 두 걸음, 드디어 호수에 도착했다.
One step, two steps, I finally arrive at the lake.

바로 저기에 보물이 있겠구나!
Right there must be the treasure!

옷을 벗고, 수영복으로 갈아입자.
Let me take off my clothes and change to swimwear.

첨벙! 물에 뛰어든다.
Splash! I jump into the water.

아이 차가워! 너무 차가워서 더 이상은 들어갈 수 없어!
Oh, it's cold! It's too cold that I can't go in anymore.

여름이 되면 다시 와야겠다.
I should come back again when it's summertime.

그때까지 보물이 있어야 할텐데...
I wish the treasure stays here until then...

그래! 여기에 안내 팻말을 세워놓자.
Right! Let's put up a guide sign here.

<호수 바닥에 보물 없음>
<There is NO TREASURE at the bottom of the lake>

이러면 아무도 모르겠지?
If I do this, no one should know, right?

난 정말 똑똑해!
I'm so smart!

민호의 눈사람
Min-ho's Snowman

이번 겨울에는 눈이 굉장히 많이 내리는구나!
It snows very much this winter!

엄마, 저 밖에 나가서 눈 갖고 놀아도 돼요?
Mom, may I go outside and play with the snow?

그래, 하지만 감기에 걸리지 않도록 옷을 껴입고 나가도록 해.
Okay, but you'll have to bundle up before going outside or you'll catch a cold.

네 엄마, 장갑이랑, 부츠랑, 털모자를 쓰고 나갈게요.
Yes, mom, I will go out wearing a glove, boots, and a fur hat

민호가 문을 열자 매서운 바람이 세차게 몰아쳤다.
As Min-ho opened the door, a bitter wind gushed up.

와! 정말 춥구나. 이런 겨울에는 밖에 있기가 정말 힘들겠어.
Wow, it's really cold. It must be really difficult to be outside during Winter like this.

밖에서 일하는 사람들도 따뜻하게 지냈으면 좋겠다.
I hope people who are working outside could stay warm.

문 밖으로 나가자, 앞 마당은 온통 하얀색이었다.
Upon going out the door, the front yard was all white.

지난 며칠동안 눈이 왔고, 민호의 발목까지 쌓여있었다.
It's been snowing for the past few days, and it's piled up to Min-ho's ankle.

좋았어! 이번 여름에 해변에서 모래성을 만들었던 것과 비슷해!
Great! This is similar to making a sandcastle at the beach this past Sumer!

여기 있는 하얀 눈으로 예쁜 눈사람을 만들어야지!
I will make a beautiful snowman with the white snow here.

민호는 눈을 모아 덩어리를 만들고, 덩어리를 굴려 더 큰 덩어리를 만들었다.
Min-ho gathered snow and made a mass, rolled the mass to make a bigger mass.

제법 크기가 커진 큰 눈 덩어리를 바닥에 고정시키고,
He fixed the mass, which has gotten quite large, to the ground.

그것보다 조금 작은 눈 덩어리를 그 위에 고정시켰다.
And fixed a mass that's slightly smaller on top of it.

하지만 아직 뭔가 부족해! 민호는 혼잣말을 했다.
But there is still something missing! Min-ho talked to himself.

그래, 눈, 코, 입이 필요하겠어.
Right, I'd need eyes, a nose, and a mouth.

어디보자… 눈은 여기있는 까망색 돌을 붙이고,
Let's see… For the eyes, I can put the black rocks here,

코는 저기 있는 나뭇가지를 사용하면 되겠지?
For the nose I can use the branches over there, right?

입은… 그래! 나뭇잎을 붙여보자!
For the mouth… Right! Let's try putting on the leaves!

하나씩 하나씩, 드디어 얼굴이 완성되었다!
One by one, finally the face is finished!

제법 사람같은데! 내 친구 해도 되겠다!
It looks quite like a human! You can be my friend!

반가워, 눈사람 친구! 내 이름은 민호야.
Good to meet you, snowman buddy! My name is Min-ho.

우리 앞으로 사이좋게 지내자.
Let's try to get along from now on.

민호야! 저녁 먹을 시간이다!
Min-ho! It's time to have dinner!

이런, 시간 참 빨리 가는군!
My, time does go fast!

눈사람 만드느라 정신이 없었네.
I was too into making a snowman.

네! 엄마, 바로 들어갈게요! 잠시만요!
Yes! Mom, I will go back right in! One moment!

눈사람 친구! 미안하지만 얼른 저녁을 먹고 올게. 잠시 기다려줘.
Snowman buddy! I'm sorry but I will be back after a quick dinner.
Hold on for a moment.

아, 그런데 너 너무 춥겠구나… 이렇게 있으면 안되겠어.
Oh, but you must be too cold… You shouldn't stay like this.

그래, 내가 방에 가서 옷을 가져올게!
Right, I will go to my room and bring clothes!

자, 여기 내 털모자도 쓰고, 오리털 외투도 입고… 따뜻하지?
Here, wear my fur hat, put on a down jacket… It's warm, right?

음… 하지만 이정도로는 충분하지 않아. 아! 더 좋은 생각이 있다.
Hm… But this is not enough. Oh! I have a better idea.

캠프파이어를 만들어 주면 따뜻하게 지낼 수 있을거야.
If I make a campfire, you will be able to stay warm.

여기에 장작을 쌓고, 기름을 뿌리고, 성냥을 켜자!
Let's pile up the firewood, put fuel, and light up a match!

화르르 - 불이 붙었다.
Whoosh – the fire caught on.

와~ 성공이다! 내가 저녁을 먹고 올 동안, 따뜻하게 있어!
금방 올게!
Yay~ Success! Stay warm until I come back after having dinner!
I'll be right back!

허겁지겁 저녁을 먹고 돌아온 민호가 앞 마당으로 뛰어나간다.
Coming back after finishing dinner in a hurry, Min-ho rushes to the front yard.

눈사람 친구! 내가 돌아왔… 이럴수가? 어디로 갔지?
Snowman buddy! I'm ba… What in the world? Where did you go?

친구야! 어디갔니? 그 새 어디로 간거야?
Buddy! Where did you go? Where did you go in that short moment?

내가 준 옷은 다 여기에 버려두고, 어디로 간거야?
You left all the clothes I gave you here, and where did you go?

캠프파이어도 그대로 있는데, 어디로 간거야?
The campfire is still here, and where did you go?

Other Titles You Might Be Interested In :

SPEAKING

LET'S SPEAK KOREAN
Learn over 1,400 Expressions Quickly and Easily w/ Pronunciation & Grammar Guide Marks.

BEGINNERS

KOREAN FOR EVERYONE
Complete Self-Study Program : Beginner Level: Pronunciation, Writing, Korean Alphabet, Spelling, Vocabulary, Practice Quiz With Audio Files

VOCAB BUILDER

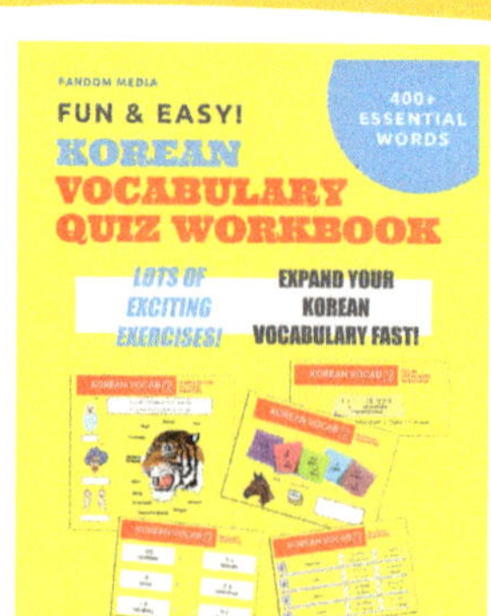

FUN & EASY KOREAN VOCABULARY QUIZ WORKBOOK
Learn 400+ Essential Words w/ Exciting Exercises

KOREAN CULTURE

KOREAN CULTURE DICTIONARY
From Kimchi to K-Pop and K-Drama Cliches. Everything About Korea Explained!

K-POP / KOREAN SLANG

THE K-POP DICTIONARY
Fully Understand What Your Favorite Idols Are Saying

Learn Korean With Classic Short Stories

With Downloadable MP3 Audio Files

English-Korean Bilingual Text

한국어-영어 대역본

Hye-min Choi

BEGINNER

GRAMMAR WORKBOOK

Let's Study KOREAN

BRIDGE EDUCATION

Complete Practice Work Book for Grammar, Spelling, Vocabulary and Reading Comprehension with Over 600 Questions

LET'S STUDY KOREAN
Complete Practice Workbook for Grammar, Spelling, Vocabulary and Reading Comprehension w/ Over 600 Questions!

LEARN KOREAN WITH CLASSIC SHORT STORIES

FOR MORE TITLES, PLEASE VIST

NEWAMPERSAND.COM

www.ingramcontent.com/pod-product-compliance
Ingram Content Group UK Ltd.
Pitfield, Milton Keynes, MK11 3LW, UK
UKHW061950290726
14090UKWH00021B/1163

9 791188 195473